Y0-DJN-682

FINISHING LINE PRESS
www.finishinglinepress.com

Widow Maker

poems by

Pamela R. Anderson-Bartholet

Finishing Line Press
Georgetown, Kentucky

Widow Maker

ISBN 978-1-64662-563-5 First Edition

Acknowledgment

Whurk: "What Color Are the Blue Ridge Mountains?"

Publisher: Leah Huete de Maines

Editor: Christen Kincaid

Cover Art: Meredith Balogh and R.E. Anderson

Author Photo: Allen E. Bartholet

Cover Design: Elizabeth Maines McCleavy

Order online: www.finishinglinepress.com
also available on amazon.com

Author inquiries and mail orders:
Finishing Line Press
PO Box 1626
Georgetown, Kentucky 40324
USA

Table of Contents

Dedicated to
Al Bartholet and Dr. Ramesh Mazhari

Widow Maker

She breaks hearts.
Snaps them in half—
pockets one piece—
sinks perfect white incisors
into the remainder.
You are tender—
delicious—to her.
Next year
she might go rogue again—
extracting your pocketed half heart
to take another bite.
You want to reclaim
this stolen piece of you—
but she just stands there—
heart in upturned palm.
You are stunned—
frozen—
and then you realize—
it is not your heart.

Prophet

Miles from home, the news is bad.
At the airport, gates fill like a bathtub,
people floating out of and into planes
while the woman wearing the hijab
paces the waiting area.
I scan my cell for another message.
In ER. Heart stopped 3 times.
Looking for blockage.
Every second counts.

Now I am encased over a wing.
The woman in the hijab settles
beside me. Glances over with sable eyes.
When I ask, she answers
with a voice as warm as a blanket
pulled from a summer clothesline.
Afghanistan. My homeland. Many years ago,
men broke into our home. Raped my sisters. I saw.

We land on a rain-slick runway. Passengers
snap to attention. Jerk bags from overhead.
Stab phones. Crush close.
She remains motionless, her hand a comfort over mine.
One night, our father woke us; guided us.
Over the mountain to Bannu. Pakistan.
When I go back, my burka hides who I am.

She pauses.
He will live.
Your husband.
He will.

The Visible Horizon

In your deep sleep, you saw no visions—crossed no bridges—
traversed no cavernous tunnels, seeking a pinpoint of pearly white.
You never levitated or hovered near the ER ceiling,
observing swift-moving hands as they passed
over your inert frame. Only later
did you see the angel. She strode into the ICU,
coat flapping like heron wings—
a sweep of baby birds fanned behind her,
each with stethoscope snaked around neck.
Her eyes were indecipherable black wells
as she listened to the beauty of your unseen heart—
its tribal beating—the ebb and flow of blood
lapping against its shoreline—your breath
as it filled the intersection between earth and sky.

Yes

In ICU, they strap left wrist to metal bar—right leg to mattress.
    I'm sorry, baby.
croons the nurse.
    Are you in pain?
    You are, aren't you?
She is brisk. Skilled.
    He needs to keep that leg straight.
    If he yanks out the balloon pump line, it won't be pretty.
You are oblivious, aware only of thrumming pain—rib cage and heart.
You nod
    Yes (it hurts)
    Yes (pain meds)
    Yes (you know I am there)
I squeeze your hand—brush fingers over your face—
wonder if you will ever again open your eyes.
    Keep that leg down.
she commands, pressing it flat.
I echo
    Down.
You comply like a recalcitrant child—lines carved between brows—
mouth slack around breathing tube.
    Yes (it still hurts)
    Yes (more meds)
    Yes (you know I am there)

Paper Cut

Big trauma doesn't eviscerate days:
        Heart attack
in the hotel lobby.
        Blockage
in the left anterior descending artery.
        Cardiac arrest
in the ambulance.

It's the solitary weeknights.
        Chinese carryout
at the kitchen counter.
        Phone calls
that go unanswered.
        Paper cut
on the index finger of my dominant hand.

High Dive

I climb to the high dive,
one rung after the next.
Countless strangers
reached the top before me
to swan dive—cannonball—
backflip—somersault.
Some ripped into the water—
others belly smacked—
a few chickened out
before standing atop
the highest platform.
I continue up and up,
ignoring my fears
of deep water and heights—
disregarding
my pounding heart—
the gathering clouds
and gusts of wind.
I turn my face to the sky,
never glancing down or back.

Metrics

Numbers drive us forward
like 2 mules yoked to a hand plow and tilling soil:
98 point 6
125 over 70
We breathe metrics, but they are nothing
when compared to hospital charts—graphs—
and attention to digits of all sorts.
34 days since the last fall
boasts a hand-written sign in the cardiac unit.
We visualize tumbles from hospital beds—slippage
from toilets unobtrusively located behind curtains—
Chevy Chase-inspired pratfalls as patients trip over IV tubing,
backsides flaring in the cheery, blue-cotton gowns provided.

And what about survivor measurements?
If my husband is one tick on the positive side of a cardiac arrest poster,
how many log into the negative column? How much faith
should we place in assurances that
90% of people with widow makers don't make it
a stat that is eclipsed only by the comment
10% don't survive

I resist this arbitrary mixing and matching of information.
Keep it on the same playing field, that's all I ask
while simultaneously making uneducated guesses on exit numbers:
58% of cardiac patients are treated and released within 3 days
24% return within 72 hours
Are those reasonable gauges?
Does the hospital CEO report similar data to boards of directors?
Are year-end bonuses awarded for positive outcomes?
We adjust the yoke and return to manageable metrics:
13 pills in the morning—3 at night
Weight holding steady at 178
8 days since the heart attack—and counting

The Sword of Damocles

He straps on his external defibrillator, and I am glad.
Glad because he still has a pumping heart that might need
a reviving jolt. A two-inch screen flashes cobalt,
displaying his name and a cartooned torso. *If it buzzes,*
he scowls, *I'm taking it off.*

He is as calm as vengeance, burning to pounce on anything
resembling prey. Unwelcome indignities have been a shock,
starting with his body's betrayal in an echo of his father's
cardiac arrest 30 years ago. Same MI; different results.
The dangling Sword of Damocles.

There are other mortifications, too. I expect him to spring a leak
from pinholes peppering his needled body. The nick
on his wrist reveals where the stent's journey began.
The perforation near his groin produced an eggplant bruise
and his observation: *Mick Jagger dreams of results like this.*

A doctor forewarned: *If the life vest goes off, you'll think a mule*
kicked you in the chest. After two blasts in the ambulance
and three in the ER, we don't want more electricity hurdling
into his heart. He falters at the edge but does not fall
onto the sharp side of the sword.

What Color Are the Blue Ridge Mountains?

...I ask my husband as we drive
east on Route 33 toward Skyline Drive
and the Shenandoah National Park.
We debate this question
as if it were the most vital issue of the day.
Dusty blue. Gray blue.
It is three weeks exactly since his world stopped
five times: Twice in the ambulance, thrice in ER.
Widow maker, a surgeon told us.
A miracle he survived, said another.
And it does seem like a miracle right now,
our car cruising comfortably at 60. John Martyn's
Solid Air whispering through the sound system. My hand
snugged into his and resting on the console between us.
Smoky blue. Shadow blue.
We don't talk about the days he lost in ICU,
plumber's auger down his throat and balloon pump
doing his heart's work.
When I explain to friends, I demonstrate:
This is his heart, I say, making a fist
with my left hand. Over the top
I wrap my right thumb, index and middle fingers.
These are his arteries.
In the webbing between index and middle,
that's where it happened. Where a speck
stoppered his heart like a cork in a wine bottle.
Ocean blue. Rain cloud blue.
I don't mention my newest nightmare:
A dog that lunged at me then snapped its jaws
around my demonstration fingers.
The way my free digits gripped its snout,
bearing down and dragging the beast toward me,
our eyes locked and terror growing.
Steel blue. Slate blue.

We drive, and I want to keep going,
past our street and up the steep, curving highway.
Past the fear that my heart might continue beating
after his is done.

Ouroboros

Across the kitchen counter
I soldier 13 bottles with pink, yellow, and white pills
that stand sentinel against another heart attack.
They appear wholly inadequate—small children
armed with squirt guns then sent into battle.

Labels are equally unimpressive, if inexplicably alluring:
    ELiquis.
    LiSINopril.
Who invents those monikers? White-coated lab technicians
huddled around a bar on a Friday night?
    MetoPROlol, suggests one tech.
    No, insists another, *MeTOprolol. Toe. Like toeing the line.*
I imagine that toeing the line is mandatory when concocting remedies
whose warnings quail even the stoutest of hearts.
    "Do not take if you have severe heart circulation
    or failure problems," reads one cautionary description.
Does cardiac arrest count? I wonder.
And what about those side effects?
    FurOsemide may cause "irreversible hearing loss."
    AmiOdarone outcomes are succinctly labeled "dangerous."

Despite dire predictions, we anchor our faith in pills
and the strangers who prescribe them.
The well-groomed doctors with glossy hair and perfect teeth—
the homely ones who look like librarians—
the ones who seem no older than our youngest child—
others who teeter on wobbly legs.
We cling to the Rod of Asclepius,
knowing it could twist at a moment's notice
into a snake that eats its own tail.

Fascination

Who can explain your fascination with dolphins?
You yearn to plunge into seawater with Spinners
or troll the Amazon with Pink River Shapeshifters.
You are captivated by their jet eyes and teeth
like strands of pearls. Their clicks and whistles.
You want to slip silently into their pod
while tributaries inside you run wild. You imagine them
lifting you up until you break the surface
with a spray of water that catches the light and heals
the tiny, shattered pieces of your untamed heart.

Invocations

Get-well cards festoon the dining room table like beach umbrellas
plugged into sand. Wildflowers, constellations, and ocean images
jostle for premium position in the limited space allotted.
They rub elbows with a plethora of comedic oddballs.
Linus, kite clenched in one grubby fist, strides purposefully
along an indeterminate scrap of land. A tubby golfer
attempts to sink a putt in a hole the size of a small car. An old man
rolls his IV stand down a hospital hallway, backside displayed
in a breezy, striped gown. Two sunglass-wearing Dalmatians
steer a blue convertible on a traffic-free highway.
Inside the cards, hand-written notes alternately soothe and brace
as friends rush to express previously unspoken sentiments,
"I love you" chief among them.
Methodists, Episcopalians, and Mennonites offer invocations to God.
Baptists start prayer chains. Catholics light candles from coast to coast.
Someone tucked a note into Jerusalem's Wailing Wall. Allah
has been praised, drums beaten, sage burnt, and positive thoughts
launched into the Universe.
I am fortified by these displays of affection and attempts at cheer,
but he eyeballs the growing hoard with skepticism, rejecting
their mystic qualities while simultaneously reluctant to insist
I stash them away. I offer a handful of newly delivered envelopes;
he slits them open and hands them back.

Mall Walkers

Women in stretch pants with coordinating floral-print blouses
and men whose pants rest high across beer guts
lead the mall-walking rehab parade with modified goose steps.
Canvas sneakers are augmented with canes, walkers, and oxygen tanks
strapped into backpacks. Bum knees and bad hips have been replaced—
hearts mended—rotator cuffs repaired—ankles braced.
Those of us who hanker to regain lost vigor are inspired
by mannequins in skimpy pink undergarments,
but no one pauses at anchor stores with mirrored windows
that reveal too much. We stagger on, eyes forward, until we hit
the goal: 2 times around equals 1 mile and the reward
of a donut from the coffee shop located near faux leather sofas
and reclining massage chairs.

In Dreams

His father appears to him in dreams.
Still dark-haired and slim—not one second more or less
than the day his heart gave out. In this dream,
they play catch on the front lawn. His father lobs the ball—
it smacks into the glove. Their eyes meet
across the distance, and each strides forward—reaches out—
folds arms across shoulders.
They perch on the front stoop—saying nothing
while spring peepers raise their voices
into the still darkness.

But this is just a dream, and the sleeper
must open his eyes to a new day. On this day,
his own sons will spend a lazy afternoon with him.
They, too, will play—one catching—the other
looking for opportunities to steal the moment.
When shadows stretch and chill air cools their cheeks,
they will pause, heads angled toward each other.
His boys will laugh and jostle each other. And he—
this man who loves his sons—will feel a warm breath
of memory drift across his face.

Charnel House Dream

The stranger haunts me. He slides
close to the pane—mutters
I can get you anytime. His laugh
slits the air like tin chimes swinging
above my porch. His hands jab out—
but the window holds. He draws close—
closer—his face pressed tight
to the glass. Our palms mirror.
My voice hangs in my throat.

Wasps

Summer heat lingers like honey over everything,
encouraging indolence but never hindering mud daubers
as they construct pipe organ nests along the seam
of our bedroom window. Unlike the two of us,
these wasps toil day by day and inch by inch.
They arrow into slender arteries with minimal fanfare,
murmuring in a low cacophony that sends goosebumps
up my spine. I lack the heart to broom them away
on chilly mornings. Why destroy such purposeful industry?
Such single-minded focus?
I avoid spider webs decorating the nook, too,
granting those ambitious artists a few extra days
before they become prey for wasp larvae
occluding the passageway.

Mercy

Dust off your alligator shoes—
shake out your best silk shirt—
and shimmy into your high-pocket jeans.
We're going dancing tonight
under a Shenandoah Blue Moon—
swaying to the blues man whose guitar
screams for mercy.

It's the only thing we need right now. Mercy
and a song that's as fine as frog's fur—
that blisters the parquet
and pleads for toe taps—hip shakes—finger snaps.
Your heart keeping time with mine
and no thought
about the way it all will end.

Listening With My Heart

I listen to his memory:
I spent the summer in Arkansas with my grandfather.
While I was gone, Dad turned the empty lot next door
into a baseball diamond.
Our supper is finished—dirty dishes still on the table
while he nurses a beer and I swirl red wine around in my glass.
I was so busy when I got back home
that I never even played on the field.
Why this story today, when August heat shoulders
into the house and sunshine casts light across the floor?
He cleared brush—beer cans—bottles people threw from cars.
Mowed it—chalked lines—put in bases and a home plate.
After I came home, bulldozers moved in and plowed it under.
Some stranger bought the land—built a house on it.
Dad never liked that guy.
Which part of this memory hurts most?
Why resurrect this pain?
He didn't think ahead. He could have called the county—
asked about the lot before he did all that work.
He could have bought it himself. But he didn't use his head.
No. He did what I do now.
He used his heart.

Galvanize

Let's galvanize your heart,
shall we? We can wrap it in zinc
and seal the seams—
barricade it against air, sunlight,
and splintered fragments of moon.
We might give it a name—
maybe Daniel or Peter.
We will say
Oh, Daniel! How are you today?
or
Good morning, Peter!
When I tap your chest,
your galvanized heart will thump back—
protected and ready for the next battle.

Healer

I drift up the stairs to the room where candles burn
and water trembles over river rock in a shallow basin.
The woman with silver-blue dreadlocks
waits near the solitary window. I tell her…

Genetics.
It's in his family.
Nothing changes heredity.

I ease onto the table as she clacks together
two hot stones.
Once. Twice. Again.
She presses them between my shoulder blades
but still I shiver. I am chilled
to the bone.

This wakes them up. So they know we are here. Sometimes
I draw a symbol on my palm—like this—
and press it against your head to calm your thoughts.

She arranges rocks on the small of my back
with hands that are sure of the work. Hands
that understand a heart can stop for many reasons.
She answers when I ask…

Long Island. I love the city. Can't believe I left.
Left for love.
My ancestors? Jamaica. India.

She pauses.

You will travel past the day.
You will unlearn the fear.

Hat Trick

These days, everyone calls you lucky.
But you don't feel lucky. That's a moniker
for heads-up pennies on the pavement
or rainbows after thunderstorms,
and that's just not you.
You're no Great Blue Heron sailing over Lake Anna
or ceramic baby baked into this year's Mardi Gras cake.
You know luck was just part of the hat trick
that saved your life—the double-triple shock
to your heart—the wire cage holding the inside open.
You lug around luck like a 50-pound sack of wet beach sand,
knowing you carry every man whose luck ran out—
who missed the boat—hung out at the wrong place
at the wrong time—strolled under a ladder
or glimpsed a black cat striding across his shadow.
All those poor, lost souls snuggle into your body,
wishing for one fraction of a second of your good luck.

Fast Shoes

Were you wearing old man shoes
the morning your heart stuttered
then stopped?
Broken-down penny loafers—
absent the penny—
or house slippers scuffed on both sides?
Where were your fast shoes that day?
Your *Timeless Style & Flawless Craftsmanship*
Allen Edmond Wingtips
with the single oak leather soles
in that luscious dark chili color?
What about your Florsheim Chukkas
or oxblood bike-toe boots?
Your waterproof deck loafers—worn sockless
in the summertime?
Surely you could have chosen
a pair of fast shoes
from all those hoofers waiting
on bamboo racks on your closet floor.
What you needed that morning
were fast shoes to help you outrun
that rogue fleck as it sprinted
down the wide-open avenues
of your heart.

How to Become a Cardiac Cripple

Feign indifference when your husband's cardiologist warns: *Don't become a cardiac cripple.*

Snicker as you saunter to the car.

Be the only one who understands his meds.

Dispense pills into blue and pink plastic containers
with weekday and morning/night dividers. Perform this task
every Sunday morning after recording his blood pressure.
Grouse when he tries to accelerate the process by asking
for meds before you double check your work. Surreptitiously
verify that he takes them daily; scold when he misses a dose.

Join him at doctor visits and nurse life-coach phone calls.

Hijack appointments with questions about diet and exercise.
Grill the pharmacist about over-the-counter meds for colds
or sinus infections. Inform your children about blood clots
discovered in his heart. Put your ear to his chest and speculate
about skipped beats. Several times a day, ask
Do you feel okay? Are you sure? Are you 100% sure?

Migrate to a Mediterranean diet.

Stock your spice rack with Mrs. Dash, rosemary, and oregano,
discarding salt, chicken seasoning, and bouillon cubes.
Buy a pocket magnifier to read sodium content on labels.
At restaurants, roll your eyes when he orders fried chicken.
Confide to the waitress that he had a heart attack.
Beetle your brows when he calls this meal his Last Supper.

Buy a family membership to a local workout facility.

Join him at the gym. Splinter sidelong glances his direction
and ask *How are you?* when he breaks a sweat. Hand him
your water bottle—cap removed. Press the back of your hand
against his forehead and insist he stop. When you get home,
tell him to put up his feet while you bring more water
and carrot sticks to cheer him up.

Keep things from him.

Don't mention increases in utility bills. Sift through mail
and remove invitations to fundraising dinners. Share
catalogs—especially Orvis—to encourage him
to think about new clothes. Screen calls and text messages.
Hover when his brothers phone to ask about his health.
Interject reminders to describe pinging sensations in his chest.

Celebrate milestones.

Bring cupcakes to his office on his heart attack anniversary.
Remind everyone that he technically worked that day,
even though his DC trip was a boondoggle. Divide
conversations into *before* and *after your heart attack*. Post
affirmations to his Facebook page. Tag friends so they
remember to send positive messages with uplifting emoji's.

Take over driving responsibilities.

Consider letting him drive when the speed limit is 35 or less
and he is familiar with every stop sign and traffic light.
Purchase two burial plots at the local cemetery. Choose
a shady spot. Drive over to visit and mention *This is our final
resting place.* When he sleeps, try to stop your brain
from re-imagining his heart attack with him strapped
to a gurney piloted by paramedics bolting into the ER.

What's Left of the Day

Crank the radio all the way up
while we blast down Route 71 to 65.
We'll drive out of Ohio and into Kentucky
then Tennessee. On the far side of Memphis,
we'll track along the Mississippi
and tool past cottonfields that watch our progress
with their shy, white faces. We will blister
into Louisiana, past its flatlands and estuaries,
driving until land drops straight into the Gulf.
When we get there, you will lean into me—
take my hand—twine your fingers
through mine—and claim what's left of the day.

Tap Dancing

Zydeco music from buskers on Royale
catches your ear, so you pause with all the other tourists
just to watch them perform
and even though it's hotter than blazes,
you can't peel your eyes away
from that sweetheart of a fiddling girl
in her cornflower blue dress with little red polka dots—
or is it another pattern?—and you edge in close
and notice the fabric is flimsy and almost transparent,
and it's speckled with ladybugs—
a sure sign of good luck—and she's sawing along
in time to the old geezer thrumming a washboard
with a spoon in each fist, sweat shining on his cheeks
and stains drenched along both sides of his work shirt,
and he's standing next to a big guy
who's squeezing the heart out of his accordion
and then—you can't make this stuff up—
a tiny boy throws down a wooden box—no more
than a 3-by-3 square—and slides grubby bare feet
into scruffy black shoes—then ties ribbons
around ankles that are so skinny they remind you
of your mother's prized china cup,
and who knows where that memory came from
because this child's skin is lovely and warm
and as brown as brown sugar and her cup
was lily white and nothing like this beautiful
mahogany youngster, who jumps onto the box,
his feet flailing and—*Hot Damn*—if he doesn't have taps
on his toes and heels and the crowd goes crazy,
people pulling bills from wallets and purses
and tossing cash into the open fiddle case and you realize
they're playing *Jambalaya*—one of your favorites—
so you grin at the kid and try to snag his attention,

but he is as serious as a heart attack
and that's when you remember
how your own heart stopped—even though it always
tapped like a champ, never skipping a beat,
much less stopping cold.
And then the sky splits apart with a soft rain that plunks
into the dusty street and onlookers scatter under awnings
then drift away but the buskers keep busking
and the kid keeps tapping and your heart keeps beating
and the whole scene does your heart good
and it pulls on your heart strings
and it thaws out your frozen, stunned heart
and you feel nothing but glad.
So very, very glad.

Additional Acknowledgments

The burning sensation in the crooks of his arms did not initially alarm my husband. When he broke out in a cold sweat, he realized he was in trouble, but getting help was tricky because he was alone in a Marriott Hotel room in Washington, DC. He remembers dialing the front desk (Henry), his room door opening, and rain smattering his face as paramedics eased him into the ambulance. But that's it.

Many people saved him that day: paramedics who defibrillated his heart in the ambulance—ER and ICU doctors at George Washington University Medical Center, including Mohammed—nurses Courtney, Nora, Ruby, Sade—and Dr. Ramesh Mazhari, who worked for 1 hour and 15 minutes to start his heart multiple times, find the blockage, and insert a stent.

There was the airline ticketing agent in Raleigh who squeezed me onto a nearly full flight to DC—the woman wearing a hijab who sat next to me on the plane—friends Elizabeth Bartz, who gave me the keys to her DC apartment, and Eric Nuzum and Katherine Kendall, who hosted our sons in their DC home during the most critical days—work colleagues Kathy Spano and Susan Rogers—our daughter, Lysa—my sister, Robin Close, who, as a nurse, cut through confusion to share what was happening in the ER. Then there were people who supported us after we returned home, especially Bo and Sandi Rose; Martha Woodroof; Bob and Tricia Brown-Leweke; Pam and Jim Huggins; Jeanmarie Badar and Jim Kauffman; Nancy Barbour and Phil Kedrowski; Matt, Karen, and Alex Bingay; and others. It was a series of lucky breaks and helping hands.

Widow Maker honors, recognizes, and thanks these heroes.

Pamela R. Anderson is a traveler, blues music lover, yoga practitioner, and former public radio fundraiser who grew up in Northeast Ohio's Steel Valley and has never owned a red bathing suit. Her chapbook—*Just the Girls: A Kaleidoscope of Butterflies; A Drift of Honeybees*—was published by The Poetry Box in 2020, and her collection of children's poems—*The Galloping Garbage Truck*—was recently released by Kelsay Books. She is a graduate of the Northeast Ohio MFA Program.

Connect with Pam at https://www.pamelaranderson.org/
Instagram: @prandersonpoet
Facebook: Pamela R. Anderson-Poet

CPSIA information can be obtained
at www.ICGtesting.com
Printed in the USA
LVHW111601120821
694951LV00002B/106